ALWAYS BE YOURSELF. UNLESS YOU CAN BE A UNICORN, THEN ALWAYS BE A UNICORN.

A Snapshot of the Weird and Wonderful World of the Tumblr Generation.

Text:
Pernille Kok-Jensen
Els Dragt
www.mare-research.nl
www.connectivityroom.com

Design:
Lilian van Dongen Torman
www.lilianvandongentorman.nl

With contributions by:
Jolijn Snijders
jolijnsnijders.tumblr.com
Into The Void, p. 45
Mingling With The Masses, p. 127

And the help of:
weheartit.com
urbandictionary.com

Thanks to MARE Research
and to Olivier Biggs for his bullshit
fllter

Cover image by:
Sebastiaan Pagano Mirani

BIS Publishers
Het Sieraad Building
Postjesweg 1
1057 DT Amsterdam
The Netherlands
T (+) 31 (0)20-515 02 30
F (+) 31 (0)20-515 02 39
info@bispublishers.com
www.bispublishers.com

ISBN 978-90-6369-350-3

ALWAYS BE YOURSELF. UNLESS YOU CAN BE A UNICORN, THEN ALWAYS BE A UNICORN.

A Snapshot of the Weird and Wonderful World of the Tumblr Generation.

ABOUT THE AUTHORS

In her teens, Pernille Kok-Jensen escaped the countryside of Denmark to rock the club scene in Amsterdam. This former stylist/burlesque dancer/editor knows her way around the global creative scene. As the Connectivity Director at MARE Research Pernille connects the dots between trends, people and brands. Even after biking to work for half an hour through the rain, you won't catch her having a bad hair day and her OOTDs are always lookbook worthy. Oh, and you can call her PJ if you want.

Els Dragt is actually really a spy masquerading as a trend researcher. Working at MARE Research, this girl has a rare ability to communicate relevant trends, without using any fancy marketing lingo. A talent that is not only appreciated amongst colleagues and clients, but also amongst the young trend students she teaches. Els is weird and wonderful in too many ways to mention. In her spare time she arranges her nail polish according to colour and sometimes she participates in experimental performances that merge badminton and electronic music.

ABOUT THE BOOK

Why do all the young ladies in my neighborhood have turquoise hair? Is Seapunk a kind of sushi? Or a new rock band perhaps? Should I be worried about the fact that my friends seem to believe in unicorns? Is Tumblr like Facebook for creatives? What's the point of blogs like POHTPOF? Is it lame to say YOLO? And do I need to learn how to TWERK?

This book helps you answer some of these questions by providing a glimpse into the weird and wonderful world of today's Tumblr generation. They are bold, dreamy and unfazed by the grim context in which they're coming of age.

They've got mad digital skills, great style, and a superheroesque outlook on life. Oh, and they all want to be unicorns. Consider this book a guide to help you become millennial-proof and maybe even understand your teenage kid, your Twittering pupils, your Instagramming girlfriend, your new hip employee or the next young customer that walks through your door.

To all the unicorns out there: perhaps you could buy the book for your parents so that they will understand that you are in fact not a freak but a part of a greater movement.

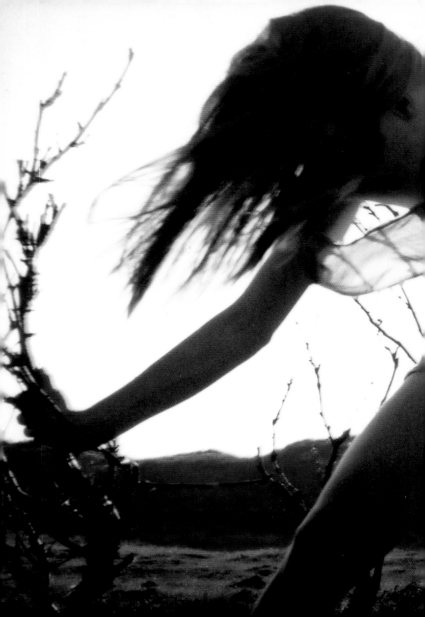

THE NINETIES CALLED, THEY WANT THEIR INDIVIDUALISM BACK

CLAP ALONG IF YOU FEEL LIKE A ROOM WITHOUT A ROOF

WHY ORANGE IS THE NEW BLACK

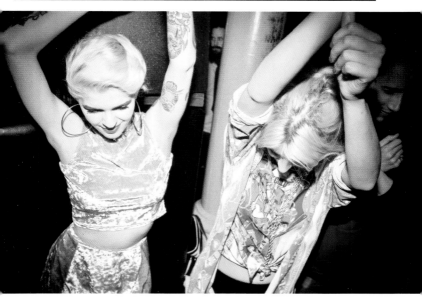

Being a buzzkill is not cool. So if you want to rebel, do it with a smile and put a smile on the face of others while doing so! Traditionally, people who wanted to influence businesses would threaten or attack them. A Carrotmob campaign, however, is when a group of people say "we'll scratch your back if you scratch ours."

The deal: make the sustainability improvements that we suggest and we'll bring our friends to your joint. Ch.Ching.Ch.Ching. Carrotmobs have already done 250 campaigns in over 20 countries around the world, from New York to Paris to Bangkok. In a boycott, everyone loses. In a Carrotmob, everyone wins!

DO DOGS DREAM?

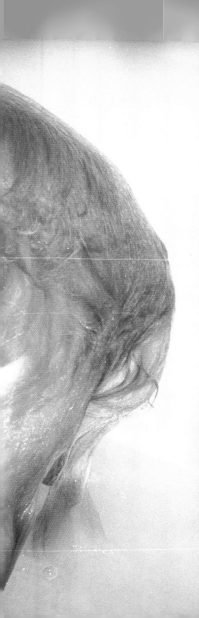

JUST ASK ANYONE

Why is the sky blue? Do parallel universes really exist? Do dogs dream? Who were those fossils again that sang 'I want it that way'? You are so lucky that all your fundamental questions in life can be answered in a split second. How did your grannies cope in the pre-Google era? Thank you so much Facebook, Wikipedia, Reddit, Howstuffworks and all other online and offline sources of wisdom. Love.

THE CHEAT SHEET TO
BECOMING SEAPUNK PROOF:

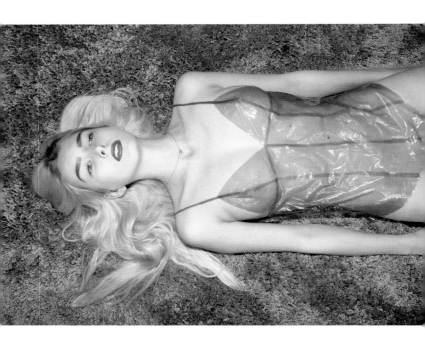

Place yourself in front
of dolphins, Yin-Yang symbols
and holographs

Get a pair of those
weird, round, mirrored
spectacles

DIY-dip-dye your hair
turquoise or pink or opt for a more
rainbow-inspired look

Be unique and dreamy
but don't you dare be hip
or trendy

Ditch your current
operating system and revert
to Windows 95

Copy and paste all
things pixelated

Express yourself
in gifs only

Smile like Mona Lisa because
you know that life is just
a whimsical little inside joke
after all

Wear sparkly leggings
(Yes boys, real Seapunks
can rock leggings)

Whisper ever so softly;
"I am actually really
a mermaid"

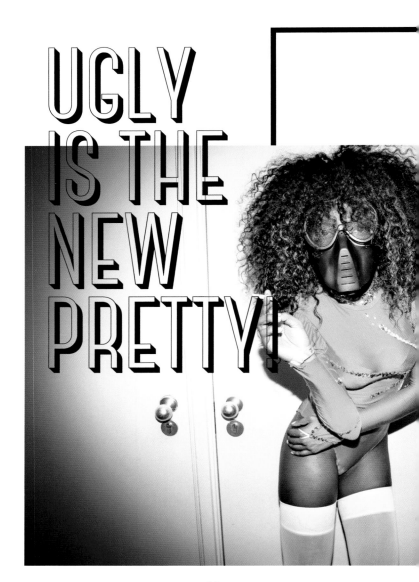

UGLY
IS THE
NEW
PRETTY!

A TASTE FOR TABOO

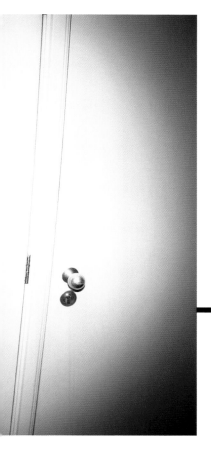

Ugly is the new beautiful.
Get yourself inked the cheap
and nasty way with a stick and
a poke – and make sure the
one who does it is not sober.
Get pink hair. If it doesn't turn out
great, fuck it! Fuck it. Get that
shiny-future-vintage-ish tracksuit
that makes you look like the
ninetees spit you out because
you didn't taste right. Direct and
uncut, bold and straightforward.
Have a Jägermeister. You are
a beautiful disaster.

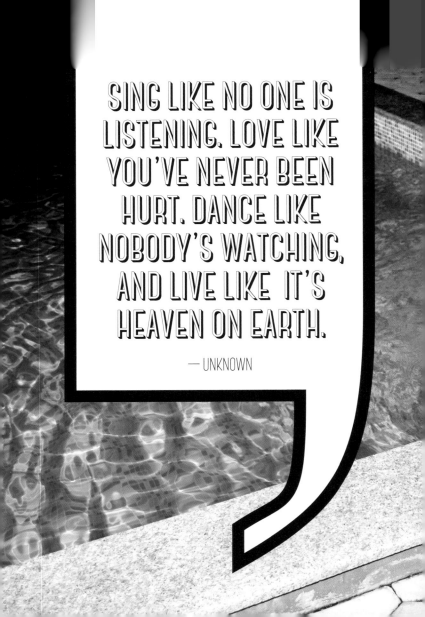

SING LIKE NO ONE IS LISTENING. LOVE LIKE YOU'VE NEVER BEEN HURT. DANCE LIKE NOBODY'S WATCHING, AND LIVE LIKE IT'S HEAVEN ON EARTH.

— UNKNOWN

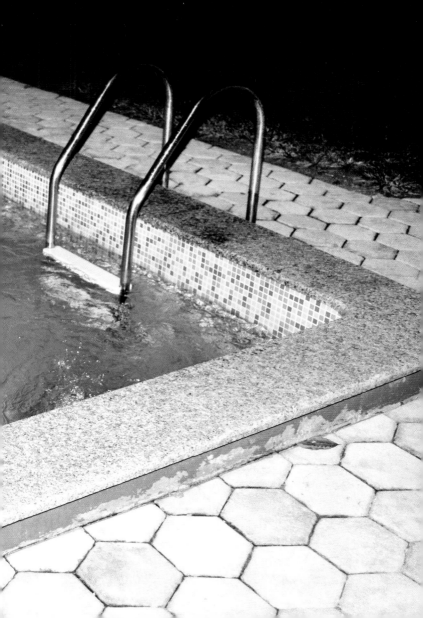

CAN YOU
SEE THAT
UNICORN
CROSSING
THE
STREET?

GO VS. SLOW

Are you on the go anytime, anywhere, 24/7, real-time and eating instant noodles while instant messaging? You must be an urban nomad living in a world where the offline and online hemisphere blend seamlessly. But stop! Can you see that unicorn crossing the street? Just freeze time for a moment, slow down, take a deep breath and enjoy. Isn't the ordinary looking extraordinary? Sigh! The fast-paced digital world is actually your companion in helping you to stop and wonder. Use the Younicornme App to turn yourself or any of your loved ones into this magical animal. Surf to the Cornify website to get unicorns and rainbows on demand, real-time, 24/7! Let's make every day magical.

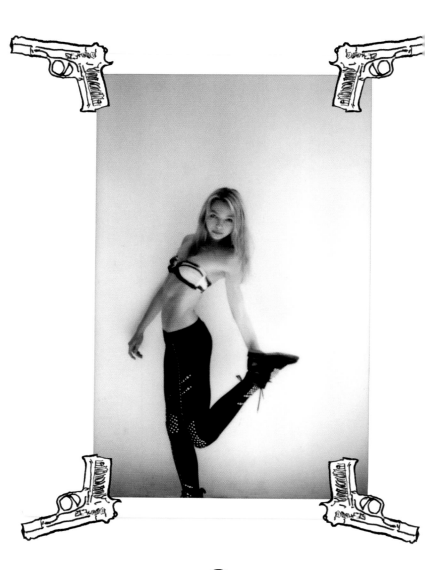

HATERS GONNA HATE

'm so totally disregarding your hostile remark. If you want to knock me down a notch you'd better step up your game. Because I know that them playas gonna play, them callers gonna call, them ballers gonna ball and them haters gonna hate. And you and I will always be friends because we love hating things TOGETHER. Oh and wait, I've changed my mind. Give me a second while I repost your remark on Facebook and Twitter. Look, we kind of made beautiful art.

FINGERS ARE THE NEW FACE

THE LIPSTICK EFFECT

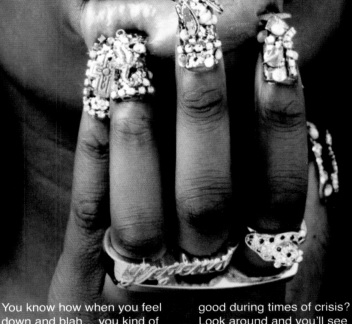

You know how when you feel down and blah… you kind of make an extra effort to at least look good? Well this is actually something like a phenomenon. Did you know that 'The Lipstick Effect' is a term used to describe how females like to look extra good during times of crisis? Look around and you'll see flocks of poor, struggling artist chicks, all with perfectly red-colored lips. Look again and you'll see that now they're probably letting their fingers do the talking.

FUCK IT WE ARE YOUNG

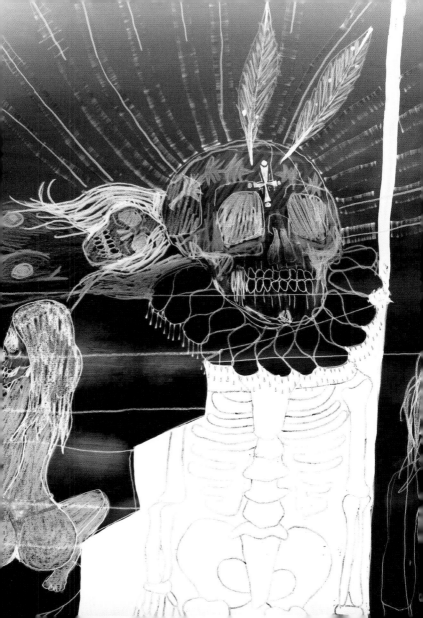

SCISSORHANDS

MOLOKID ESCAPES THE DAILY ROUTINE OF BUENOS AIRES AND DITCHES THE COMFORT OF DIGITAL RETOUCH PROGRAMS BY MEANS OF HIS COLLAGES. VINTAGE MAGAZINES, PAPER CLIPPINGS, GLUE AND SCISSORS ARE HIS SAVIORS.

Who's cooler; Leandro Pasquariello or Molokid?
Molokid is the cool one! He is here to have a good time. Leandro earns his money working and Molokid spends it on magazines, glue, different kinds of scissors and more! But at the end of the day one can't live without the other. One love.

Analogue collages? Haven't you heard of computers?
I love-hate computers. Actually, what I do has nothing to do with them. What I do has to do with going back to the roots Handmade collages are spontaneous, risky, more fun than just cutting and pasting in Photoshop. Computers have made everything too easy.

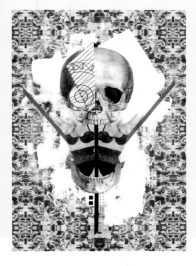

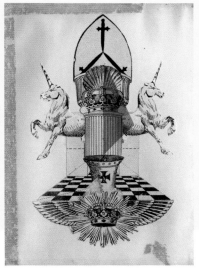

**What's up with your skull
fetish?**
Actually, this skull fetish is
more about an interest of the
human body. Every single
part of our body is so perfectly
designed. It´s such a perfect
machine, so complex!

What do you believe in?
I believe in love, happiness,
joy. I believe in destiny. We
are all here for a reason.

The spirit of youth is…..?
Always love what you do no
matter what people say.

DEAD PEOPLE BE LIKE WHATEVS

TILL DEATH DO US PART

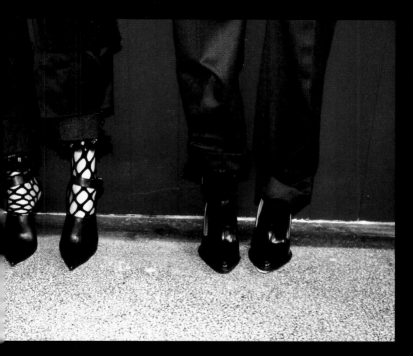

"Check out my funeral dress for today. Goodbye great-uncle Keith. May you rest in peace. We will never forget you. <3" What's so lowbrow and despicable about taking selfies at a burial of a loved one and posting these? It's a miniature family reunion, an occasion to dress up, and you get way more likes and hearts and a lot of Facebook sympathy for your loss. Do you agree or disagree with the outrage of CNN, Huffington Post and Business Insider!

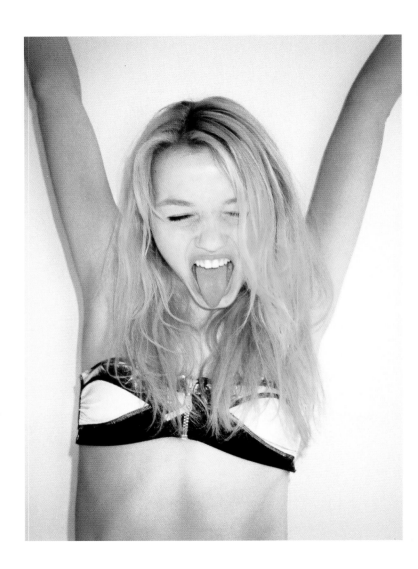

UNSELFIE

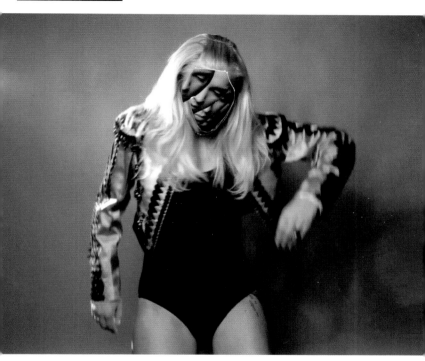

You're not still duckfacing your way through life are you? Selfies are so last year, unless you're either doing them at a funeral or making epic ones like Ellen DeGeneress' Oscar selfie.

The future is all about the unselfie. Cool, because a kick-ass unselfie lets the world know that you're hotter than your best angle AND that you're so smart, you only use Facebook and Instagram ironically.

I DON'T KNOW WHERE I'M GOING BUT I'M GOING

ARE YOU COMING WITH ME?

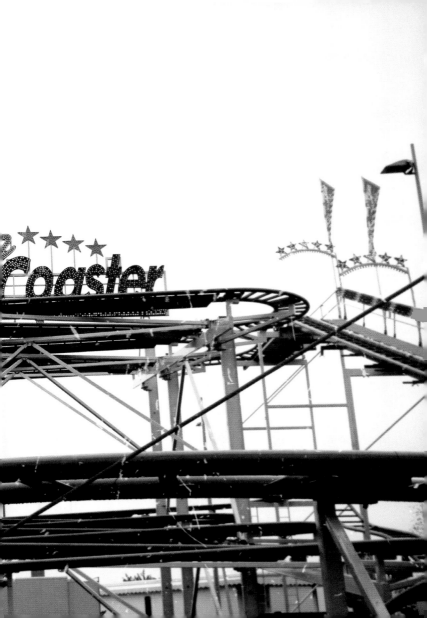

IT'S ALL
GOOD

THERE'S SOMETHING ABOUT MOLLY

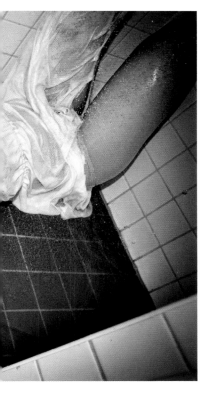

Got methylenedioxymeth-amphetamine? A bit of a mouthful to mumble on the dance-floor... That's why kids like to call it Molly – aka MDMA. The party drug is hitting dance floors everywhere. Why? Because life is bigger than the screen of your iPhone. All you want to do is escape the stress of daily life and just dance. You're obviously jonesing for interaction on a deeper level – minus the mobile. So, go ahead: excuse yourself, go out there and kiss the sky. Or better yet, take a cold shower in your favorite party outfit like our friend Joya here – minus the drugs.

WHAT'S THAT SMELL?

MY SHOE
OR YOURS?

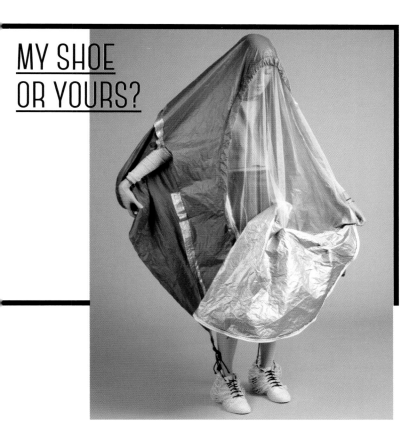

The music stops. The rain starts falling. The. Party. Is. Over. Now you have to walk a flippin' 50000 miles to get to your tent. Oh the number of times that you wished you could magically transport yourself home, Wizard of Oz style, by clicking your heels together and saying "there's no place like home"! Well, salvation is here. Now watch your friends' jaws drop while you unfold a freakin' tent from your sneaker. How's that for a party trick.

IT'S NOT A HOBBY MOM, IT'S MY JOB.

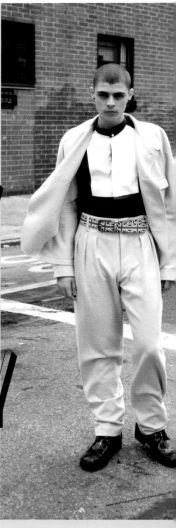

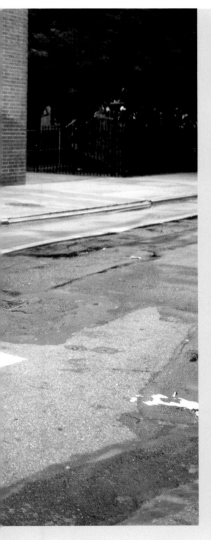

BILLIONAIRE BOYS CLUB

What'd you say? You're not a billionaire yet? Haven't invented a cure for any fatal disease yet? Pfft! You should've been a teenage tycoon years ago. You know: a free agent living their passion and upgrading the world, making a buck while doing so. With a motto like "A job doesn't define me, what I fight for does."

Damn, you make things matter. Meet Adam. At 19 he bought a camera off eBay for a couple of bucks and catapulted it into space attached to a balloon and making the most beautiful pictures of the stratosphere you can imagine. NASA peeps were blown away since they spend millions each year on high-tech satellites. So get your ass off the couch and start your empire!

TO TWERK
A DEFINITION

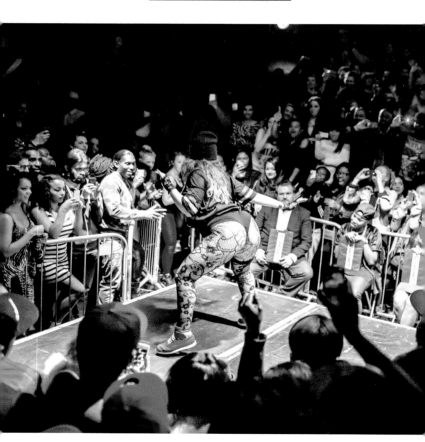

The rhythmic gyrating of the lower fleshy extremities in a lascivious manner with the intent to elicit sexual arousal or laughter from one's intended audience.
Example: "Hey girl, let's twerk on the dance floor.

To work one's body, as in dancing, especially the rear end.
Example: "She was twerking it on the dance floor."

Ghetto dancing
Example: "When I get hammered tonight,
I'm twerking my heart out."

A fancy word for 'booty-poppin'
Example: Person 1: "What if twitch was twerk and twerk was twitch?" Person 2: "HELP, MY EYE IS TWERKING!"

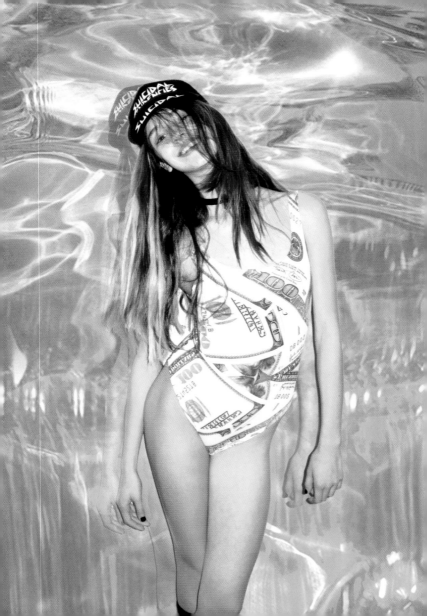

SEAPUNK IS NOT A SUSHI

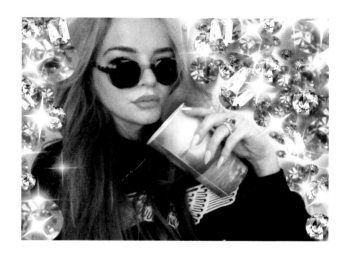

Mash together dolphins jumping through hoops, rave culture and miscellaneous 90s Internet imagery such as SpongeBob and Vanilla Ice. Now add the obligatory psychedelic orbs flying over computer-generated waves. Finally, (for that extra layer of thick irony) sprinkle with sparkles and inject with narcotic energy. Congrats! You just made a Seapunk visual. Now translate this look to your closet, your Tumblr and your everyday behavior and you'll be surfing through 2014 in a highly pixelated frenzy of uber-hip ugliness. For those of you who don't really get it, don't worry. It's just one big inside joke anyways. Just fake it till you make it.

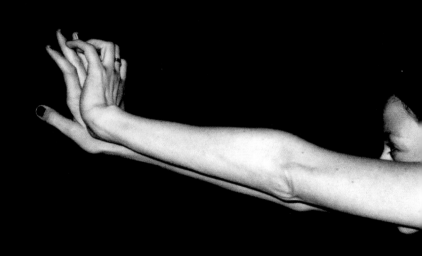

INTO THE VOID

I refuse to enjoy anything or anyone, because my eyes are wildly open to see the point of it all, which is absolutely none at all... There is no happiness, there is only a dream state of happiness... I have a hole in my body that is growing rapidly, expanding more every day. Soon that hole is going to grow so big that it will cover my whole body and consume me. I will disappear completely, to become as invisible as I already feel in this city.

HELP MY EYE IS TWERKING!

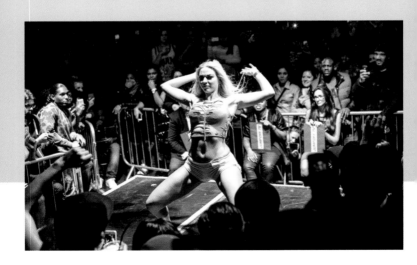

TWERK-OFF

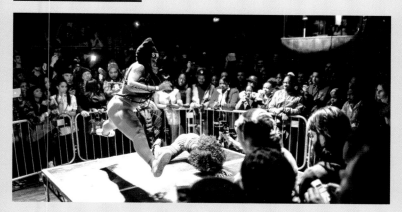

Oh yeah… so THAT happened! 2013 was the year that Miley Cyrus did her awkward VMA performance, tongue hanging out and all. 2014 was the year that she made the cover of Vogue. Now, was that in spite of the aforementioned performance or because of it? No one really knows. In any case, twerking has moved on from being a has-been viral buzz to a full-on real-life event. What? You haven't yet experienced a live twerk-off? Aawh, you poor thing, because you haven't lived until you've sat front row at a twerking championship and wiped a contestant's butt sweat off your face. These chicks are the real deal. A little bit punk, a little bit gothic and a little bit scary. Want more than the so-called interactive kicks that your iPhone can provide you with? Then get yourself the hottest tickets in town and experience some girl-on-girl action gladiator style.

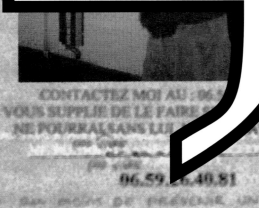

MAN IS LEAST
HIMSELF WHEN
HE TALKS IN HIS
OWN PERSON.
GIVE HIM A MASK,
AND HE WILL TELL
YOU THE TRUTH.

— OSCAR WILDE

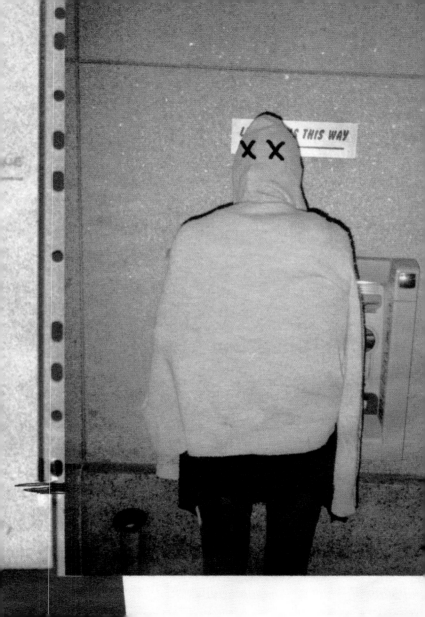

SRSLY,
TL;DR,
APOLS.

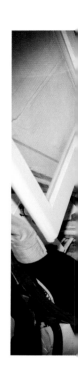

THE SHORT STORY

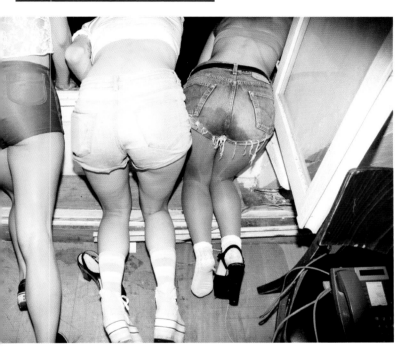

So, your mother learned how to use WhatsApp? Great, now she's texting you messages that could double as entire novels. Don't these old folks get that abrevs are saving you valuable time? The appropriate reaction is to text back: Srlsy, TL;DR, Apols. If any archaic figure might not understand this, just tell them these words have been approved and added to the Oxford Dictionary. Hope you didn't find this text tltr...

MR. POKESMAN

Do what you love. Love what you do?
My thing is making hand-poked machine-free tattoos.

How do you start a lifelong career of poking people?
One day I did one for my colleague and from then on it all started. I'll poke anything until I work out my own style.

Everyone has tattoos these days. You in it for the money?
I don't have a single tattoo… yet! All of my tattoos are made absolutely for free or on barter terms. The main idea is to show that not only the tattoo design can be cool, but also the whole setting around it: the place where the tattoo is made, the instrument used, the entire process and the result, of course.

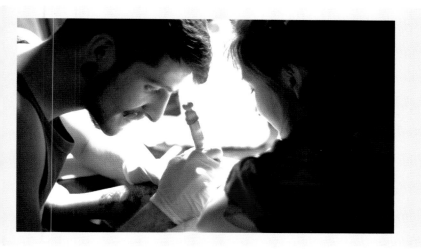

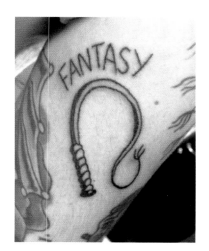

4

What you do stays with people forever. So, how do you market yourself?
I can't draw, but I consider ugly tattoos to be beautiful, anyways. I'm inspired by DIY-style tattoos, jail tattoos, Tebori tattooing techniques, ethnic tattoos and I love solid black.

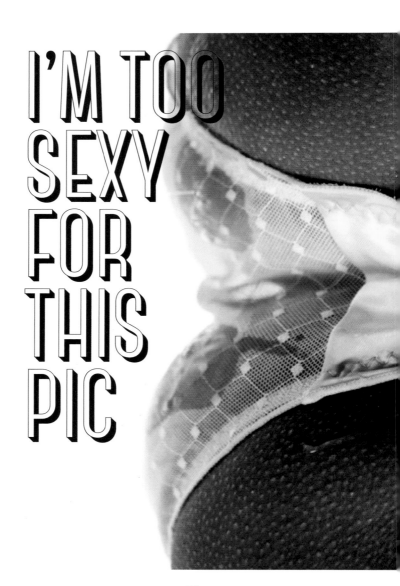

I'M TOO SEXY FOR THIS PIC

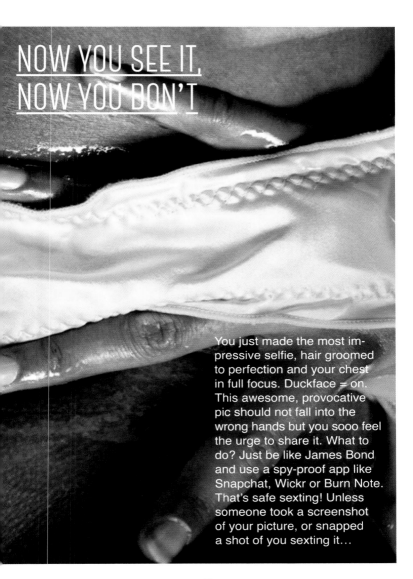

NOW YOU SEE IT,
NOW YOU DON'T

You just made the most impressive selfie, hair groomed to perfection and your chest in full focus. Duckface = on. This awesome, provocative pic should not fall into the wrong hands but you sooo feel the urge to share it. What to do? Just be like James Bond and use a spy-proof app like Snapchat, Wickr or Burn Note. That's safe sexting! Unless someone took a screenshot of your picture, or snapped a shot of you sexting it...

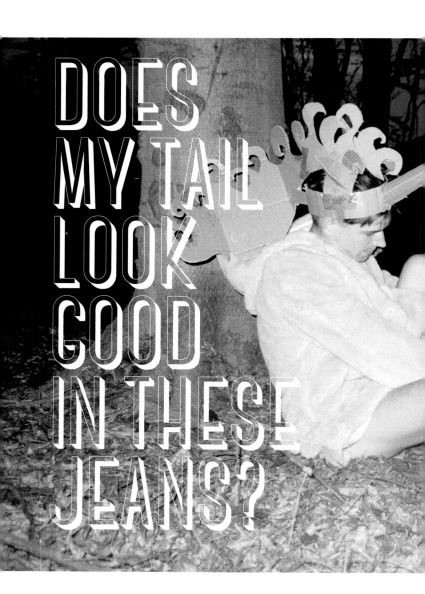

DOES MY TAIL LOOK GOOD IN THESE JEANS?

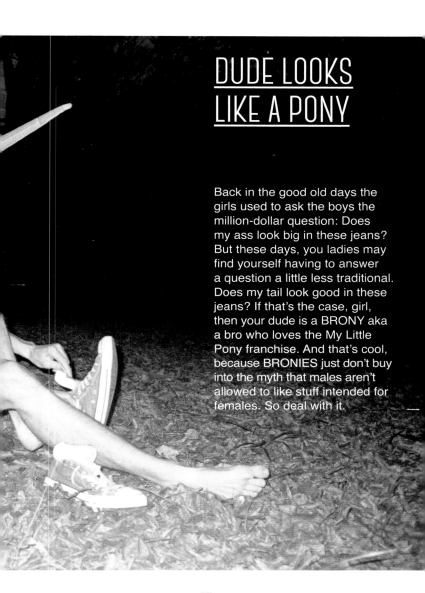

DUDE LOOKS LIKE A PONY

Back in the good old days the girls used to ask the boys the million-dollar question: Does my ass look big in these jeans? But these days, you ladies may find yourself having to answer a question a little less traditional. Does my tail look good in these jeans? If that's the case, girl, then your dude is a BRONY aka a bro who loves the My Little Pony franchise. And that's cool, because BRONIES just don't buy into the myth that males aren't allowed to like stuff intended for females. So deal with it.

I'M ACTUALLY REALLY A MERMAID

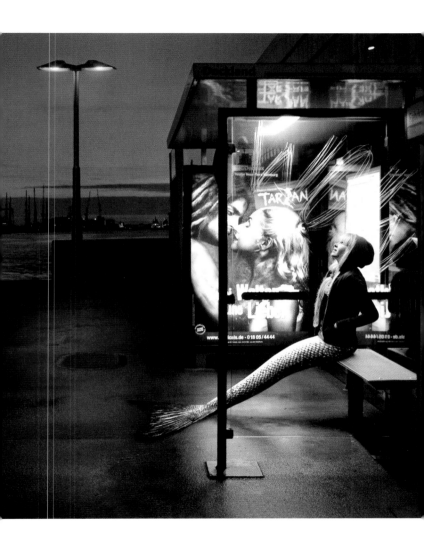

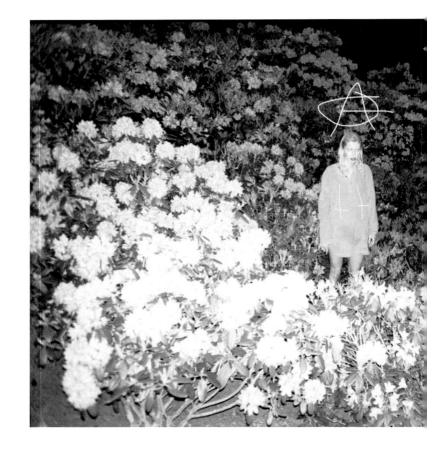

BLENDING IN IS THE NEW STANDING OUT

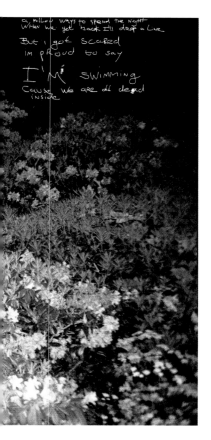

Are you tired of trying so hard to stand out? Everything and everyone is mass indie anyway and it seems impossible to be unique by rocking the eccentric. Lucky for you, stylized blandness is the new cool. Normcore, baby! Here's how it's done: put on some sparkling white athletic socks and a taupe fleece zip-up. Make collages with pictures of Jerry Seinfeld, Larry David, Steve Jobs and a touch of President Obama on casual Friday. In other words take your pick and dress up like a 'famous dude stuck in the 90s' and LOL while the media discuss whether Normcore seriously is becoming a trend.

ALWAYS BELIEVE YOU ARE GOLD

ALL THAT GLITTERS

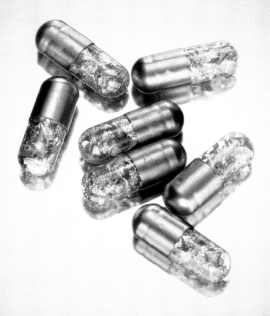

Not having a good day? Swallow one of these placebos and you'll be golden. Literally. For those of you out there who have managed to dodge the crisis, Tobias Wong and Ju$tAnother Rich Kid have produced a 24-karat capsule that will set you back $425. The rest of us, who have everything except glittery poo, will just have to DIY it in the arts and crafts section. This is much more than a placebo. This is the coolest way of always looking for the silver lining.

MISTAKES ARE PROOF THAT YOU ARE TRYING

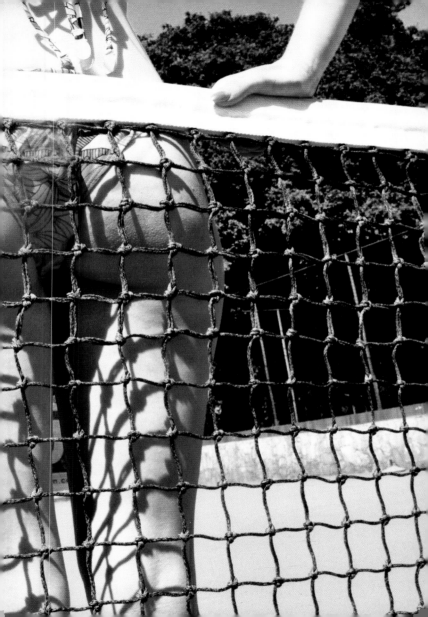

FAILURE
IS NOT
FINAL

THE NEW F-WORD

Is life giving you lemons? Are you facing setbacks? Like, EPIC FAIL? Well, let me tell you, failure is like going to the dentist: uncomfortable but inevitable. Don't be sad, wipe your tears away, push your fears and turn those sour moments into sweet ones. Because nothing succeeds like failure.

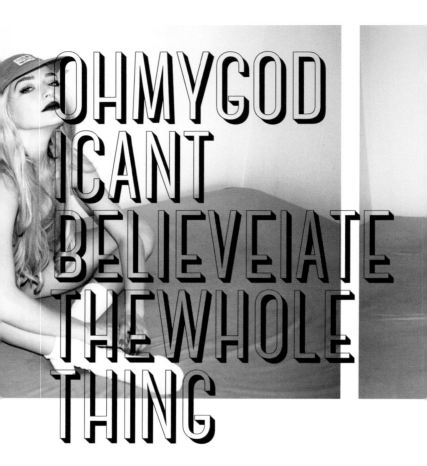

OHMYGOD
ICANT
BELIEVEIATE
THEWHOLE
THING

POHTPOF

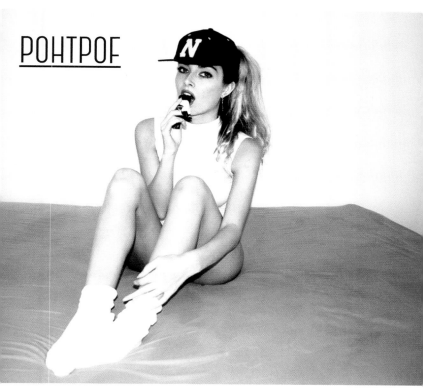

Jonesing for your daily shot of food porn? Are you someone who never sits down for a meal without being ready for your close-up? Then you've probably been featured on the POHTPOF blog. POHTPOF? Yeah, you know, *Pictures Of Hipsters Taking Pictures Of Food.* The POHTPOF movement takes food fetish to the next level. If you want to join, just start snapping away at your friends while they snap away at their about-to-be-consumed meals. It's a bit weird but, who knows, maybe with the help of POHTPOF we'll finally find out who really stole the cookie from the cookie jar.

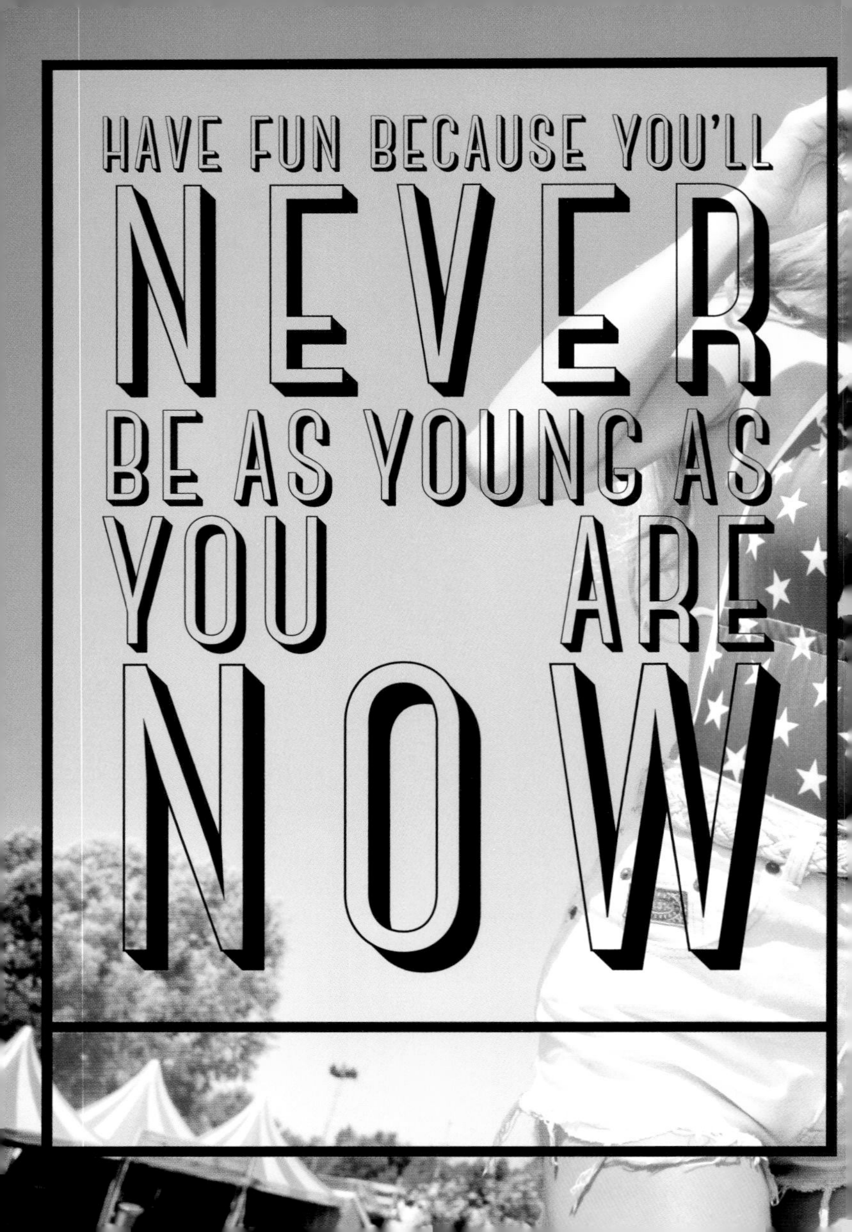
HAVE FUN BECAUSE YOU'LL
NEVER
BE AS YOUNG AS
YOU ARE
NOW

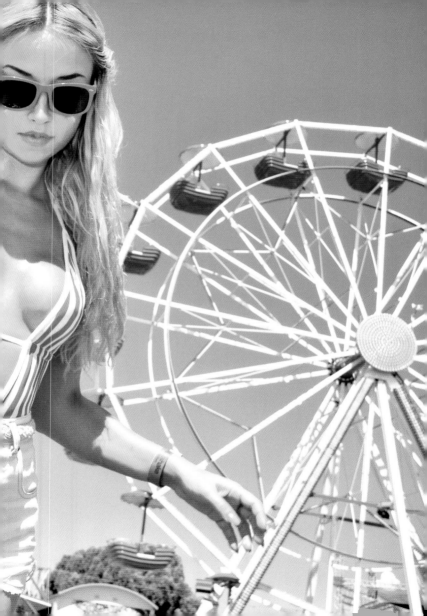

24/7 BULLSHIT FILTERS

AVANT-EVERYTHING

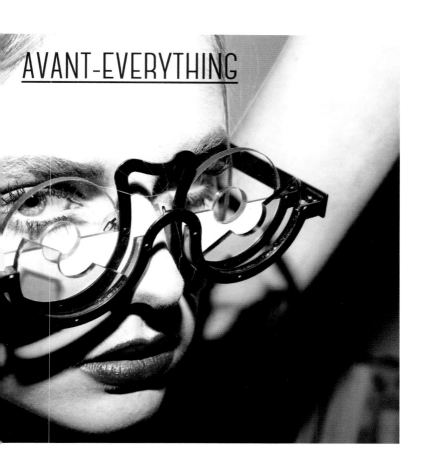

Don't you just love to hate these front-runners that are always in the know aaaaages before you? They seem to be in sync with every latest arrival or special edition. Instead of whining away, use them to your advantage.

They curate the crap from the chaff until there are only diamonds left. So follow, like and heart these avant-garde types and you'll have a 24/7 bullshit filter on hand.

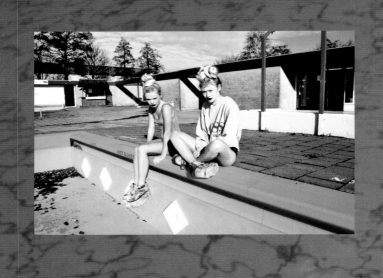

FLOATING

Sometimes when I look around it's like we're all aimlessly drifting through mid-air. In a constant state of sleepwalking. I search your faces, hoping to find a spark of truth in your eyes. The lights are on but there is no one home. But then the flash goes off. And for a moment you're all smiles, good angles and duckfaces galore. Only in that instant – when the moment is frozen in time – do you look alive. But once the light from the flash has darkened, you tune out again. Is this what we've become? Air bubbles just floating around waiting for the flash of an iPhone camera to go off, to light up our souls.

IN SEARCH OF THE PERFECT LOOP

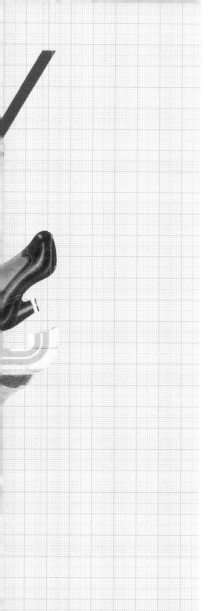

GIF ME MEANING

How are you feeling today? Do you have a case of the Mondays or are you super super excited? O Rly, OMG, LOL, YES! NO! Rofl. Fail. Booty had me like… Get your point across and shout it out with a GIF. It's perfect for communicating any of your life scenarios. A GIF is worth a billion words. Let's search for the perfect loop.

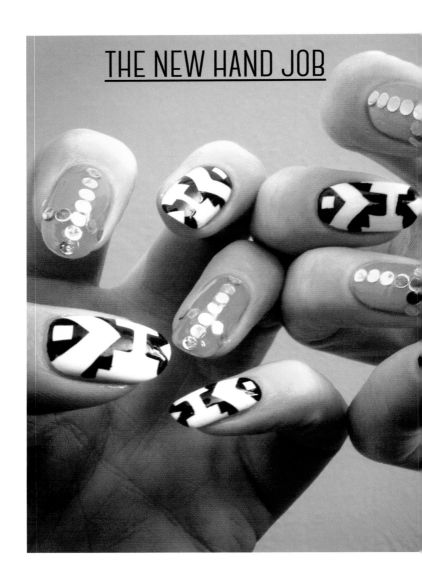

THE NEW HAND JOB

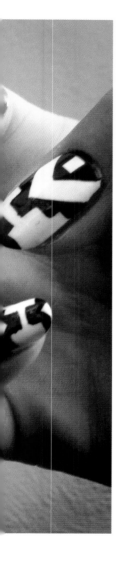

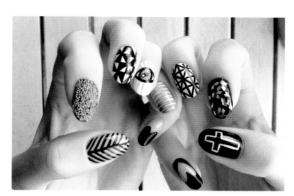

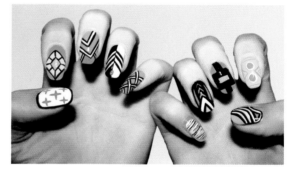

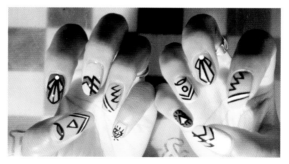

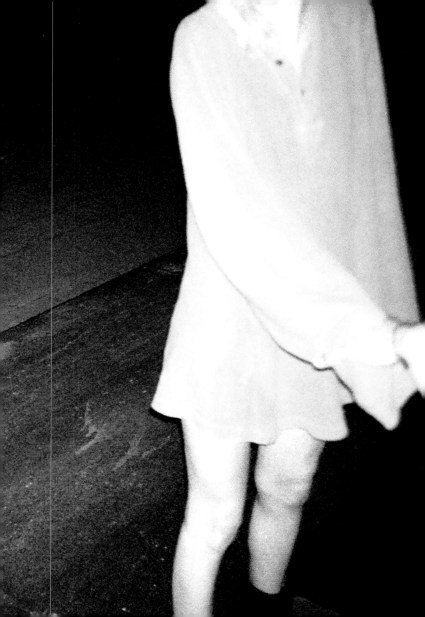

ICONOGRAPHY PORNOGRAPHY

MEET QUEEN BEE, TUMBLR JUNKIE, PHOTOGRAPHER AND FOUNDER OF I LOVE FAKE MAGAZINE AND LOLITA MAGAZINE JOLIJN SNIJDERS.

Guns, skulls, tits and tats. What gives?
They are just easy and pro-vocative symbols that every rebellious teen can relate to. A drunk guy with a shaved head showing his new stick and poke tattoo, a ten-year-old boy holding up a shotgun, a nude girl and boy French-kissing. Those are just some examples of how you can create instant iconic and timeless images on the spot, wherever you may be.

Instant Iconography?
Someone pressed 'fast-foward' and I'm making the best of it. As one of the million love-children of the Internet, I feel entitled to use its iconography. In my work, I play with the same symbols and aesthetics over and over again.

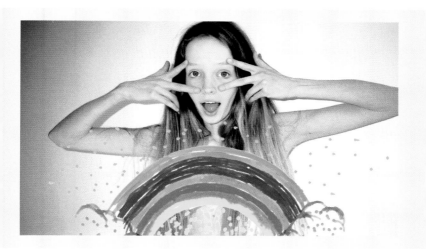

Secret to your success?
Adaptation. Although, success is just a concept that is highly overrated by society as being the most important thing in life which I now know to be complete bullshit.

Depressed much?
For me the key to creativity is the right dose of unhappiness. Right now I'm pretty happy, and hence workwise unsuccessful.

The spirit of youth is...
Unattainable, 4ever, wasted, obnoxious, depressing, loud, rebellious, $$$, visible, online 24/7, anonymous, activism, blind, hopelessly romantic, obsessive, sosexy, an asshole, nostalgic, not giving a fuck, full of life & my imaginary friend that I can always relate to.

Do you believe in unicorns?
No. But I'm obsessed with witches.

I AM
WHAT
I COPY

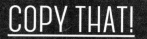

COPY THAT!

Of course your Chanel bag is fake (or rented). That's why it matches your Tumblr full of reblogged visuals and borrowed quotes on life wisdom so well. Don't you agree that imitation is the sincerest form of flattery? Copyrights are so yesterday. Copyleft thinking is the epitome of modern living. So keep dropping those mashups and show the world your remix manifesto. Besides, everything worth doing has already been done anyways.

DROP IT LIKE IT'S HOT

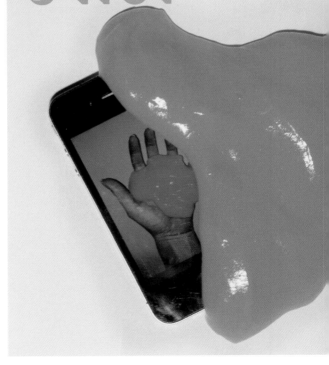

BEAT UP YOUR CELL PHONE

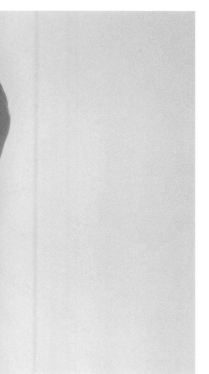

When you're checking your phone for that oh so important Twitter update while on the go, accidents can be just around the corner. So now your new cell's screen is decorated with a spiderweb pattern. But no need to shed tears; you just got yourself a kick-ass phone scar. It's like the mobile version of ripped jeans or an unshaven face. It gives you street cred because it's raw, subversive and just kinda cool.

Not rebel enough to crack your own phone? You can download cracked-screen wallpapers for your phone to show off. Mad street cred is just an app away.

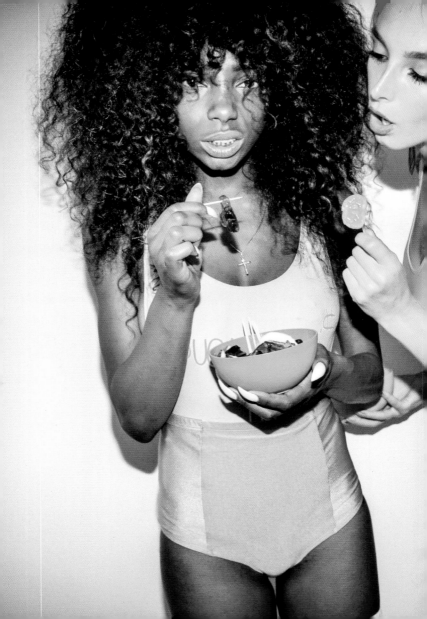

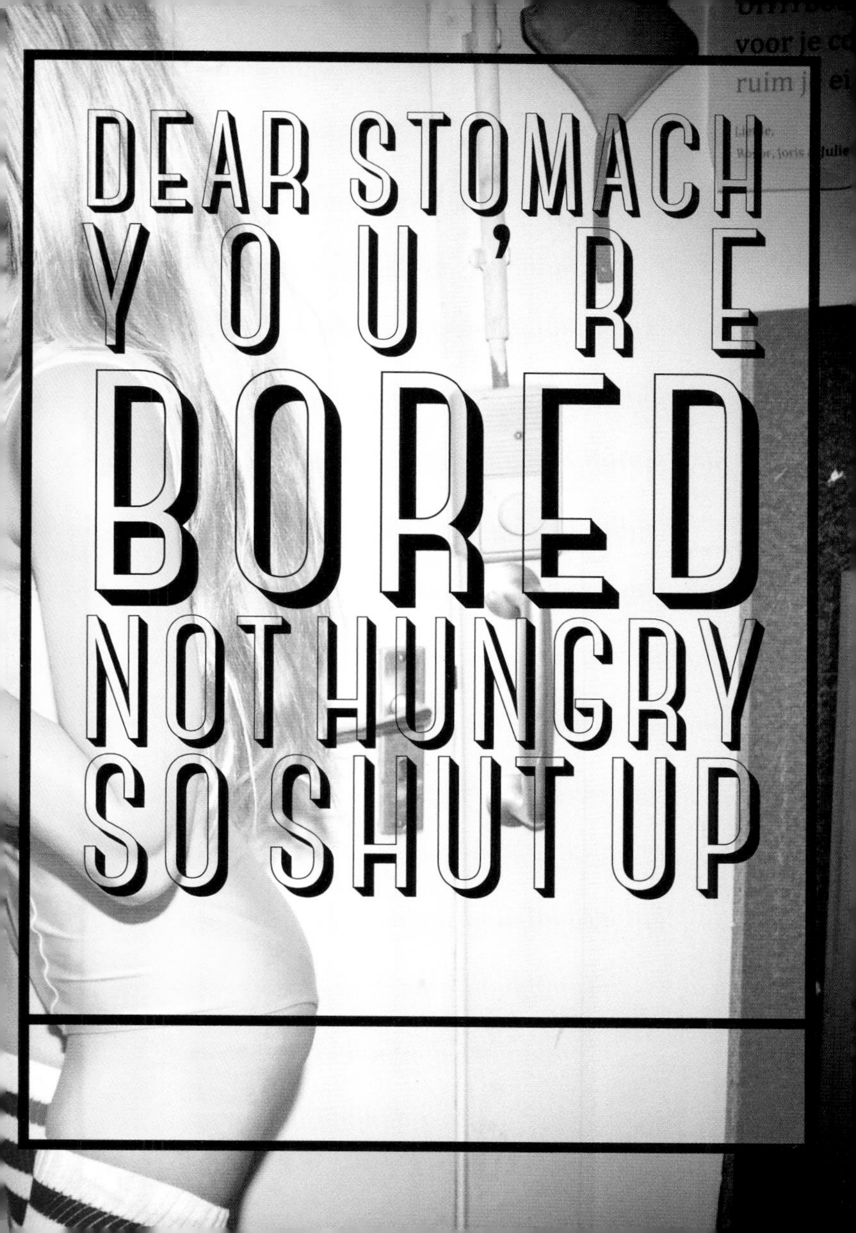
DEAR STOMACH
YOU'RE
BORED
NOT HUNGRY
SO SHUT UP

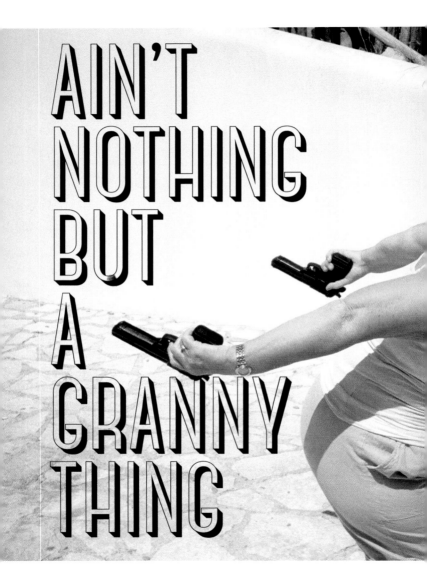

AIN'T NOTHING BUT A GRANNY THING

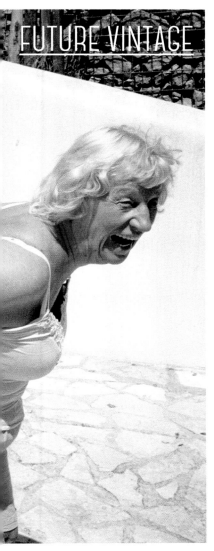

FUTURE VINTAGE

Who are your heroes? Think about it for a minute. Chances are your older sister has inspired you more than the kendalljenneruniverse.tumblr ever will. Do you prefer taking style cues from your granddad rather than from the One Direction boys? Do you find yourself ripping off your nana's steeze because she's cooler than Rihanna? Do you have a Polaroid of your parents from way-back-when hanging in your room? Just imagine your dad channeling Ziggy Stardust. Envision your mom rocking a crop top and Dr. Martens before they became hipster code. That shit is the real deal and you know it. Look around and you'll find these personifications of vintage very close to home. Ask them for advice on life, ask them to teach you some eighties moves, ask them if you can inherit their old vinyl collection. Dare them to share stories about some of the crazy shit they did when they were young. Bring them along to the club sometime to show the other kids what future vintage is.

REAL LIFE IS NOT THE SAME AS FACEBOOK. YOU CAN'T GO AROUND POKING PEOPLE.

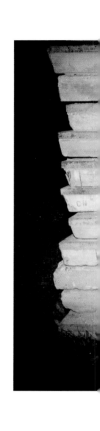

DIRTY WALL

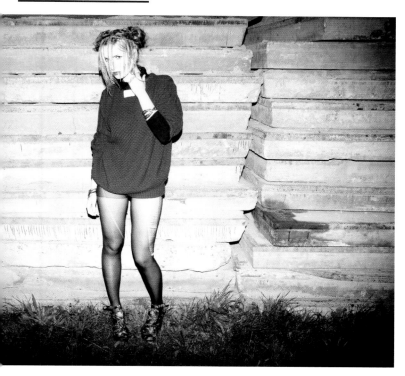

Facebook is a dirty medium. You love it and hate it. And you know it won't be long until brands will be offering you $50,- for your profile info. Are you for sale? Some say it's a matter of time before you'll be moving on to a cooler, more underground and non-commercial platform. But after leaving all those digital crumbs, will you ever have a clean slate again?

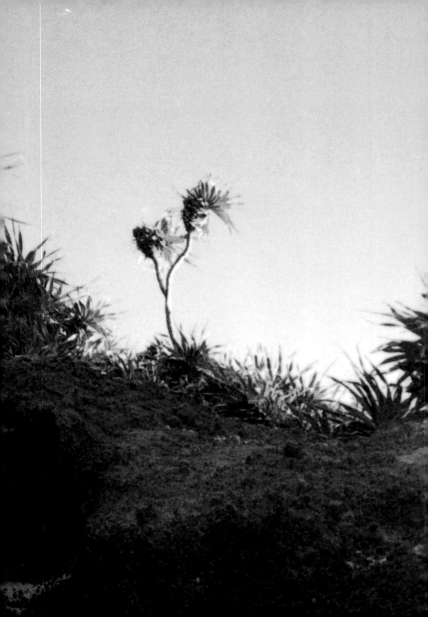

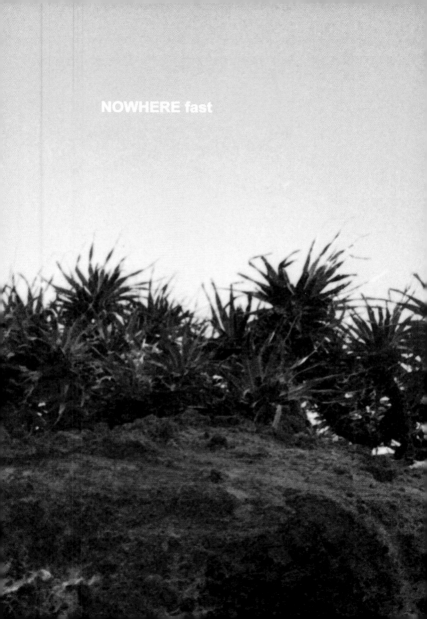

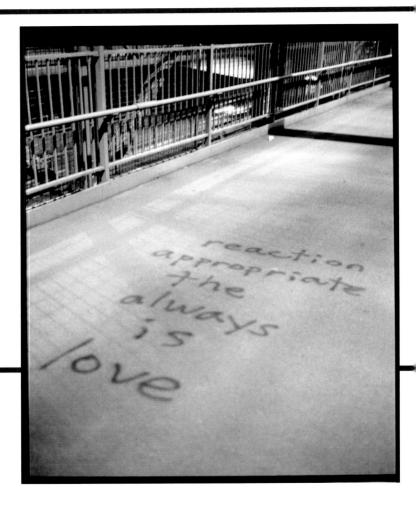

ANALOGUE AGAIN

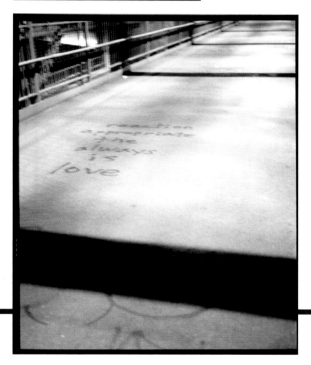

Turn off the tech. Go analogue again. Go waaaay analogue. Take a vacation from your tech gadgets. Build your own pinhole camera. Give yourself just one chance to get the perfect shot.

And when the result reveals itself, love it for all its imperfections and for the rare fact that it's a one-off. You know, sometimes you have to go old-school to go new-school.

NEW GAME. NEW RULES. LET'S PLAY!

YOUBELIKE GAME ON!

Bleuhhhh, all this talk about economic recession, planet Earth going to shreds and your parents announcing they will be going their separate ways. Let's escape, play and act like a kid! Life is a game and you are the main character. Simply walking from A to B seems like such a drag. So, let's turn this sidewalk into a jumpy trampoline. And a dreary bus ride into a Pac Man game. An ugly parking lot could be a jungle of wild flowers planted by throwing seed bombs. Hey, that dull statue over there could sure use a splash of colour. Why don't you knit it a pink hat?

TAKE ME TO BED OR LOSE ME FOREVER

INSTACRUSH

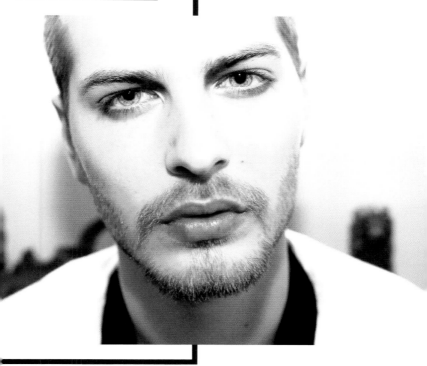

We were raised never to judge a book by its cover but what other way is there, really? The Glimpse app seems to agree that a picture is worth more than a thousand words.

This dating assistant shows your Instagram pictures. Swipe away through dozens of Instapics. Like what you see? Match! Finding your Instacrush has never been easier.

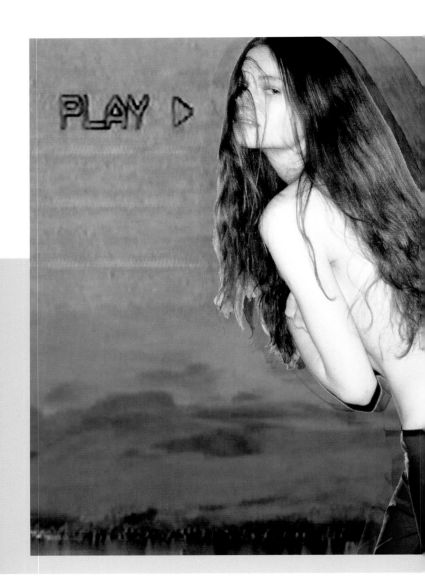

HELLO ACCESS!

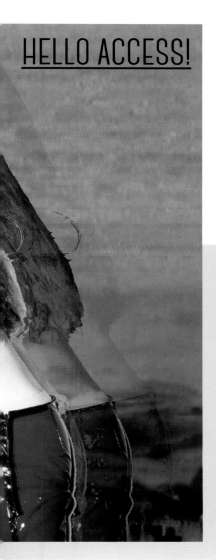

You know that owning Gucci's newest full-grain leather tote bag is not the height of status anymore. Neither are those crazy Kanye West Air Yeezy 2 Red October sneakers. And when is the last time you bought an album? Or paid to watch any kind of video content? Giving access to anyone of value to others is the new prestige. Are you using Swapstyle, iCloud, Skillshare and ZipCar already? Oh sorry, did we catch you at an inconvenient time with these questions because you are couchsurfing your ass around the globe? Goodbye ownership, hello access!

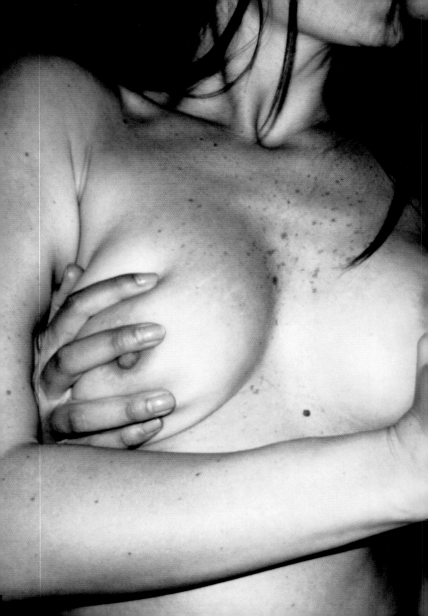

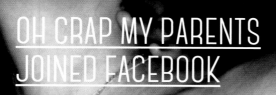

OH CRAP MY PARENTS JOINED FACEBOOK

So the cat's out of the bag. There's a party called Facebook and your folks just crashed it. Your life is officially over! They are oversharing and unloading megabytes of personal, unimportant data. Your mom is writing stuff on her own wall. Waaaah! TMI. Now what? Defriend and give them a Moleskine diary as a birthday present.

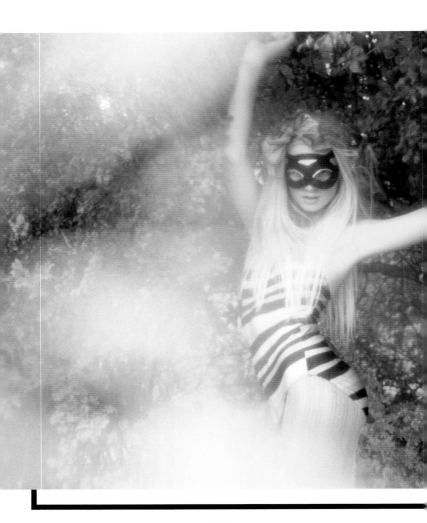

MASQUERADE

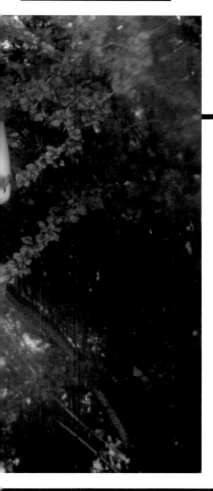

Match your outsides to your insides. Wear a mask and embrace your magical alter ego. It protects you from spying eyes, and during the cold winter months it even keeps you warm. Make an everyday mask, a fantastical mask, an animal mask, a glitter mask or a scary mask. Wear it playing your weekly badminton match, while sitting in a meeting with your boss or shopping for groceries.

TEE-TIME

ONCE UPON A TIME, A GROUP OF RIDICULOUSLY GOOD-LOOKING FRIENDS TOOK PARTYING TO THE NEXT LEVEL. THEY FORMED A COLLECTIVE, TOOK A HEAD-COUNT AND THE ECLECTIC ELEVEN LIVED HAPPILY EVER AFTER.

Why a collective?
There is strength in numbers.
And 'collective' just sounds cool.

What happens when the music stops?
When the music stops in one place, it begins somewhere else. That's one of the reasons why there is so much work for us as a collective.

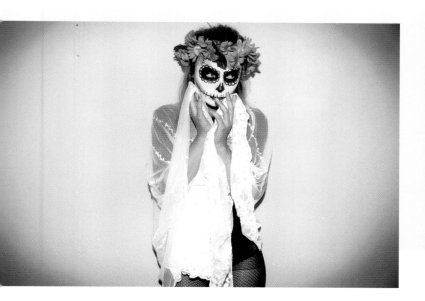

Is there a life after partying?
TEE is not all about partying. All the kids are either students or hard-working people with a lot of ambition to make it in their field.

The spirit of youth is…..
Doing a damn somersault on stage if you feel like it.

What do you believe in?
What we're doing is not going to change the world, or have a major impact on anyone other than ourselves. But we love doing it, and that's enough at this point.

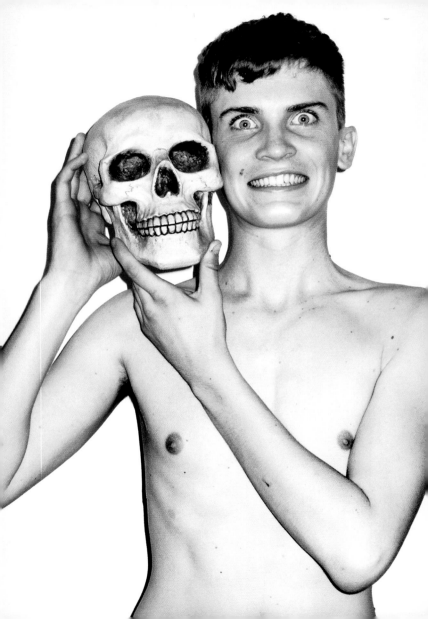

SPPPRRRRIIIIIINNNGGGGG BRRRREEEEEEAAAAK

Sometimes letting my hair down and flashing my tits at partying strangers simply won't do it. At this point, I need something more. Something big to jolt me out of the boredom with daily reality. I'm going to need some pink ski masks with unicorns on them. I'll also need a bit of Britney Spears - preferably mixed with Skrillex. I may even need cornrows. In short, what I need is Harmony Korine's version of Spring Break.

My surroundings #belike the movie version of trance music, with liquid scenes flowing in and out of each other. Give me some room, please. I grant myself permission to be pulled into a fever dream of sex, violence, and materialism. Don't worry, I'll only stay there for a little while. Lost in that magic space where the real and the synthetic collide. I'll feast off the layered, chopped, screwed, and digitized. Come, let's hover over the past and the future until there is only now. Now forever.

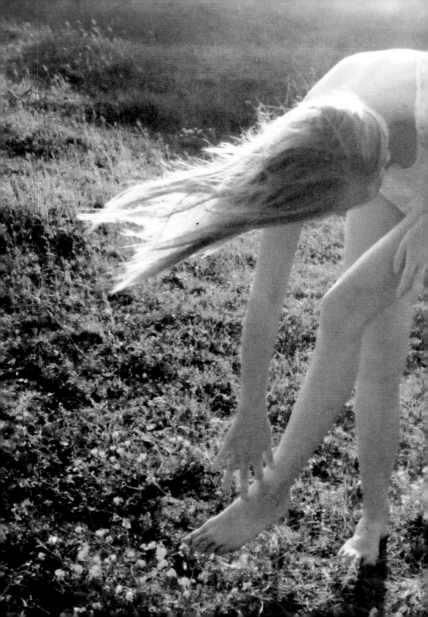

#NOFILTER

Instagram is helping everyone around the world, including you, to feel like a pro photographer. Slam some filters onto your snapshots and just like that you are the new Annie Leibovitz or Anton Corbijn. Meanwhile, in another part of town, real pros are using #nofilter to show off that they can make fabulous pics the natural way. Have you ever used the #nofilter claim, when you actually did use Lo-Fi, Toaster or Sierra? Don't be a Filter Faker. If you're going to fake it, just own it!

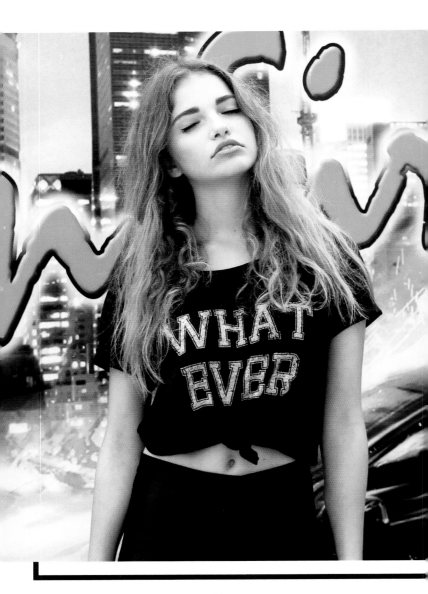

CLICKING FOR WHALES

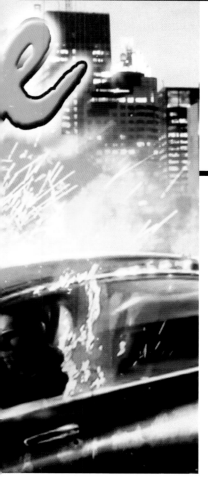

Oh my gaaawd, gay marital rights? Like! Save the wales? Click! Oh nooo, another oil spill? Grumpy face. Well, how come the grey generation keeps babbling about the new generation not caring enough about major world problems? And that while you are putting so much effort into clicking as fastas you can and keeping a keen eye on the variety of your online charity portfolio. Clicktivism is hard work.

SHOES SPEAK LOUDER THAN WORDS

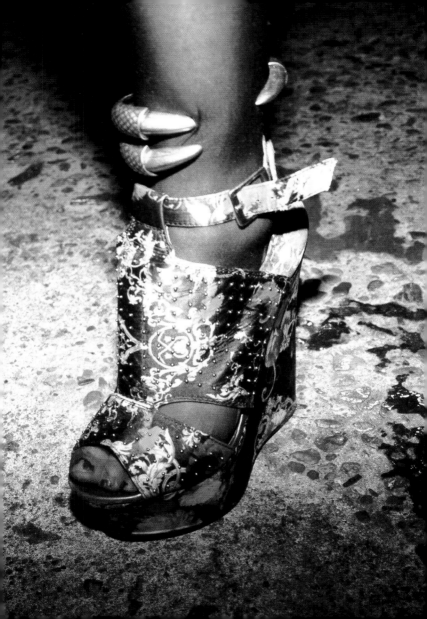

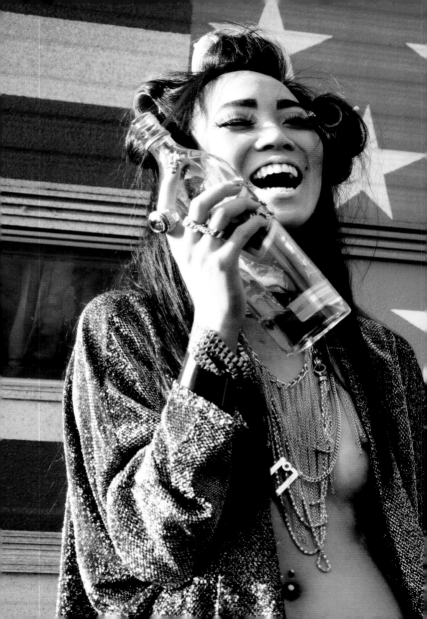

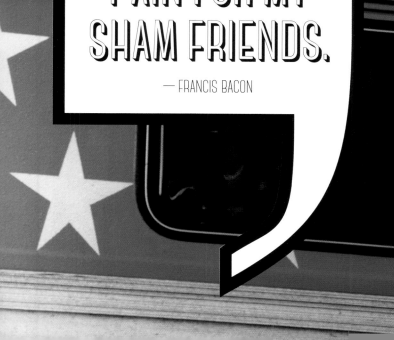

CHAMPAGNE FOR MY REAL FRIENDS, REAL PAIN FOR MY SHAM FRIENDS.

— FRANCIS BACON

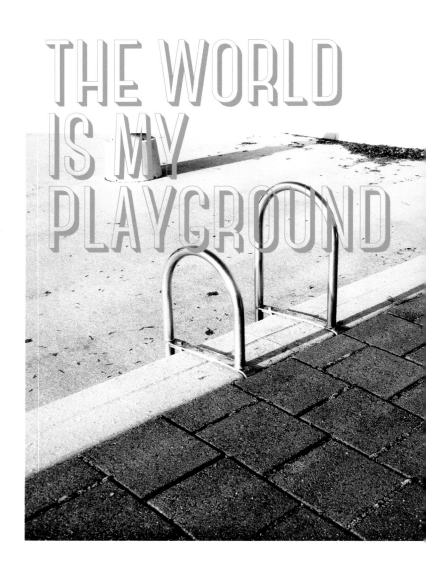

THE WORLD
IS MY
PLAYGROUND

URBAN HACKTIVISM

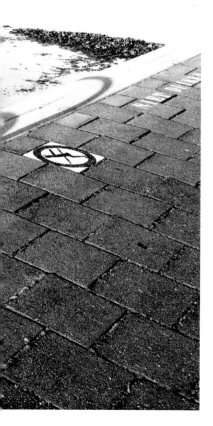

Ever come across one of those messages; *Your hair looks lovely today!* If you do, then you understand that when the city speaks, people listen. So say something back. Leave your message, secretly in the dark of night or openly in broad daylight. Reclaim the concrete garden and plant new seeds. Reinvent your offbeat suburbia. Be a guerrilla urbanist and reuse the space. Bend it, divert it and be the mastermind of your own environment. Make a mobile crosswalk carpet, plant a flower or set up a street library.

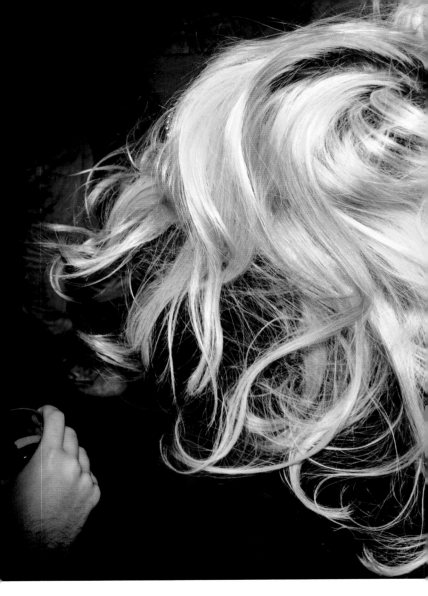

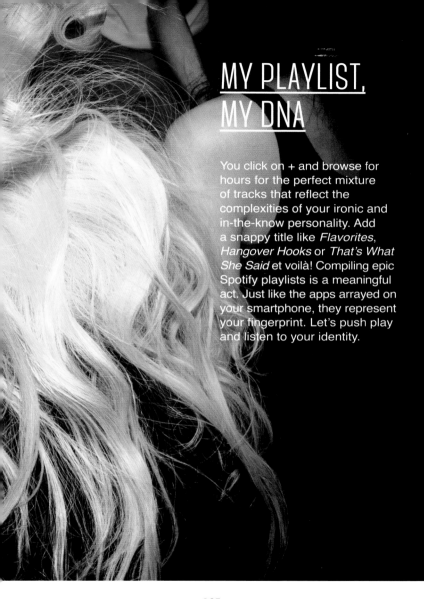

MY PLAYLIST, MY DNA

You click on + and browse for hours for the perfect mixture of tracks that reflect the complexities of your ironic and in-the-know personality. Add a snappy title like *Flavorites*, *Hangover Hooks* or *That's What She Said* et voilà! Compiling epic Spotify playlists is a meaningful act. Just like the apps arrayed on your smartphone, they represent your fingerprint. Let's push play and listen to your identity.

IF IT IS TO BE IT IS UP TO ME

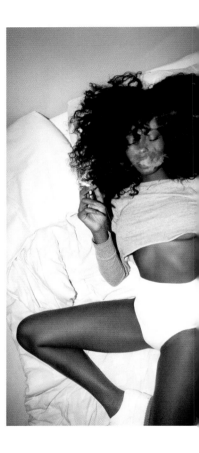

I AM WHAT I CREATE

Were you also raised by a team of cheerleaders, who kept telling you that you could be President, a rock star, an astronaut… In an interview Nicki Minaj repeats the ten little words that she was raised to believe in: If it is to be, it is up to me. The pressure! Ok, in her case it may have driven her to become a cartoonesque megastar, but for most mortals the sky really isn't the limit after all, now is it? At best, you'll get to create virtual avatars of yourselves with CVs boasting talents like waiter/model/stage kid/brand consultant/actress/blogger/CEO. Pretty awesome right? The only problem is that the whole world has the same impressive track record. And by the looks of Facebook and Instagram everyone is looking really hot while doing what they're doing. Hey you! Get off FB, go out there and earn your Unihorn!

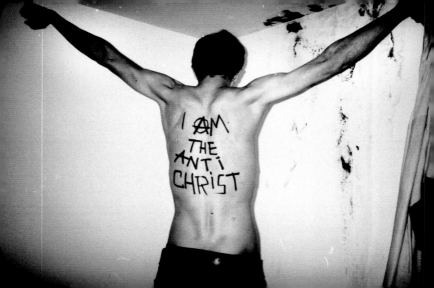

MINGLING WITH THE MASSES

At some point in our prepubescent lives we all experience that micro Socrates moment where you stop to think and ask yourself crucial questions about life; and it is those little fundamental moments in your life when you really stop to think and get all philosophical. Then a jerk named Society hijacks those thoughts, censors them and takes control. He locks up your sense of reasoning, throws away the key and keeps you busy with all sorts of repetitive activities, persuading you to stop questioning, to blend in as much as possible, advising you to match your fellow inmates as much as possible. Gradually forcing you to live life mindlessly numb without doubt. I call that purposeless. We go on living, working, fucking and breathing, passively agreeing with anything set out for us by others? So call me malfunctioned, ready to be sent in for repair work, I have a hard time bowing down to a senseless life without reason. To be terrifically frank, can I honestly just say I still don't get the punch line of life, or did I miss the memo?

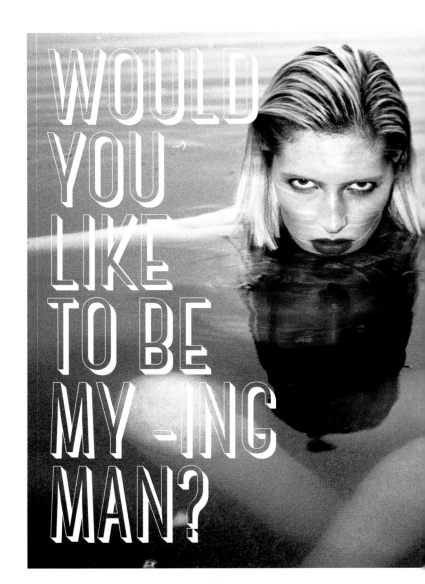

-INGING IT

Planking, Whaling, Milking, Owling, Tebowing. You can 'ingify' anything nowadays and make it the latest Vine or YouTube craze. To give you a 101 on creating your own –ing meme: pick a public place, pick a peculiar posture or activity, film it, share it, own it!

It's a shame the word Flamingo doesn't really lends itself to be ingified, otherwise it would most def be a worthy contestant in the running to becoming the next -ing. Then again, it is an awesome pose and you can totally visualize the potential of Flamingo-ing going viral, right? Flaminging!

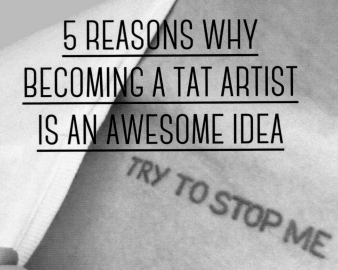

5 REASONS WHY
BECOMING A TAT ARTIST
IS AN AWESOME IDEA

TRY TO STOP ME

It's Crisis-Proof

If people want it they'll get it, crisis or no crisis.
And there are enough 'students' out there who will ink
you up for free if you provide the 'live' canvas.

The Industry is Huge

Pretty much everyone has one (one in four Brits
or Americans between the ages of 18 and 50, to be exact).
You could bring your gear to family parties and poke
away at relatives for a few extra bucks. And now that ugly
is the new pretty you could even get drunk yourself
while doing it.

A Skill for Life

Now that poke and stick is a big thing, pretty much
anyone who doesn't mind a bit of ink and blood on their
hands can do it.

It's Sociable

If you're a people's person, this is the job for you.
If not, then perhaps you should consider something that
requires less chatting about "the story behind the artwork"
or "the ironic pun intended"...

Hipsters will love you

Just because tattoos have gone mainstream, doesn't
mean they will ever go out of style.

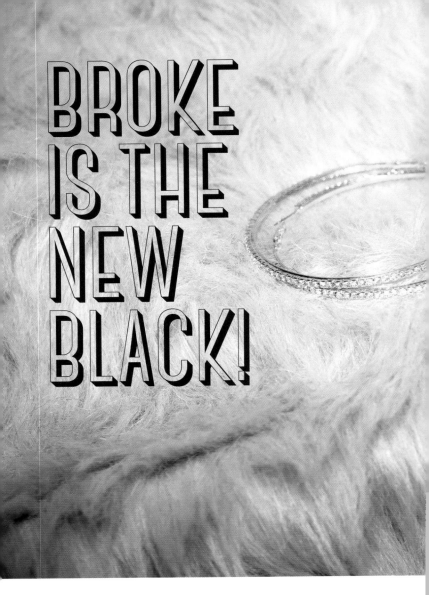

BROKE IS THE NEW BLACK!

ON PUNK COUTURE

Can we all just agree that when some kid without a dime to his name puts a chain on a brown paper bag and draws a Chanel logo on it, it's très chic? But when Karl Lagerfeld does the same to a freshman Pratt backpack and asks a whopping $3,400 for it, it's just stupid. His version may have graced the pages of Vogue, but it will only be our very own DIY versions that hit the streets.

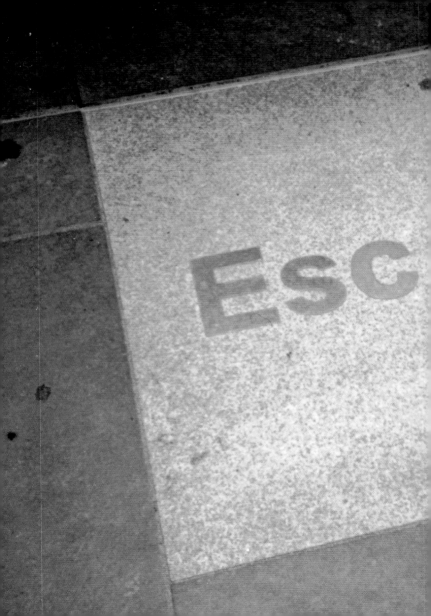

SOMETIMES
I WISH I COULD
JUST STEP ONTO THE BIG
ESCAPE
BUTTON

DO TRY THIS AT HOME

THE GENUINELY PHONY

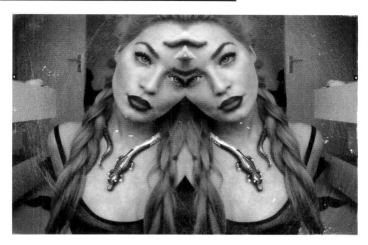

Authenticity? Yawn! Internet sensation Lana Del Rey, aka Lizzy Grant, is the perfect poster girl for 'keepin it fake' at a time when the 'real' can be manufactured. For starters there's the fake name, the fake hair, the fake ghetto princess nails, the huge fake lips and the sultry 60s Indie music sounds, or as she likes to call it "Nancy Sinatra Sadcore". Everything about her is a copy of a copy of a copy. But you know you totally want to be her. Del Rey rocks because she transcends genre. In fact, there's no one else out there just like her. The secret: only those who truly know who they are and what they like are capable of representing this by copying others. Do try this at home without the supervision of an adult!

ROCK
THE BOAT
ROOKIE

<u>ANNA WINTOUR'S PANTIES IN A TWIST</u>

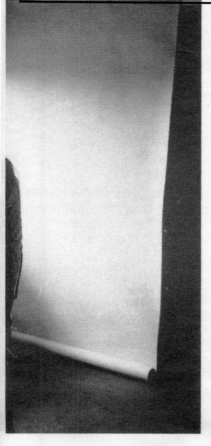

Tavi Gevinson has been the new cool kid on the block ever since she started her fashion blog, *The Style Rookie*. Thanks to her genius sense of style she quickly became a million-hits-a-day-must-see web destination. She started blogging at the tender age of 11 and boy is she good. Tavi was just the first of a growing group of young uber-talents, who are finally getting their voices heard (front row and centre) thanks to online platforms. So, the next time your parents start rolling their eyes when you speak passionately about your latest whimsical idea, tell them to listen up instead! Don't they realize that this very idea may very well be the cure to cancer or the key to a sustainable world. Tavi made Anna Wintour break a sweat – and for that she is an eternal hero. Now it's your turn to decide: which boat are you gonna rock?

IMAGES

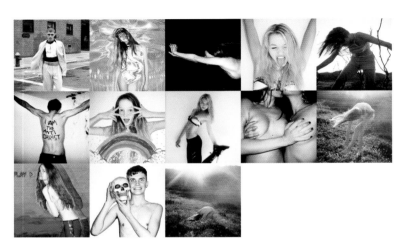

JOLIJN SNIJDERS
jolijnsnijders.tumblr.com

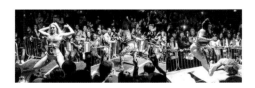

TOM JOHNSON
UK Twerking Championship
www.tom-johnson.co.uk

JUST ANOTHER RICH KID
Kenneth W. Courtney &
Tobias Wong & Koij Yano
www.justanotherrichkid.com

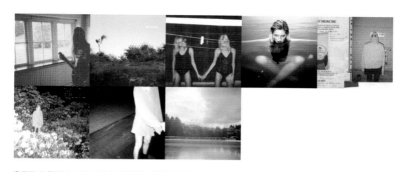

SEBASTIAAN PAGANO MIRANI
paganomirani.tumblr.com

SALTO ARCHITECTS
www.salto.ee

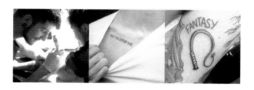

MR. POKESMAN
mrpokesman.tumblr.com

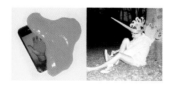

DALIAH SPIEGEL
daliah-spiegel.com

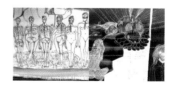

VINCENT VAN DE WAAL
www.vincentvandewaal.com

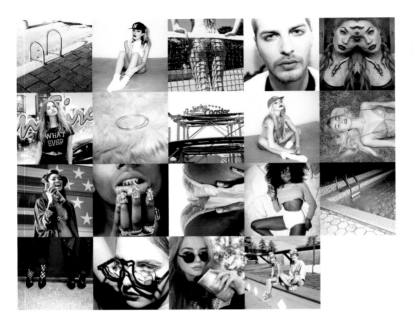

CARLIJN JACOBS
www.carlijnjacobs.com

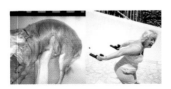

DANNY BOY
www.dannyboy.nl

JULIE PIKE
www.juliepike.no

MOLOKID
www.molokid.com

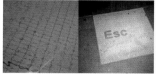

MENNO KOK
www.mennokok.nl

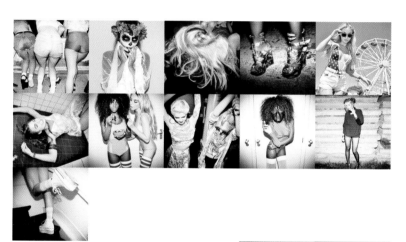

WALTER VROEGOP
waltervroegop.tumblr.com

PAULUSHAUS
www.paulushaus.net

HANA VOJACKOVA
www.hanavojackova.com

ELZA JO
House of Orange – Elza Jo
www.elzajo.com

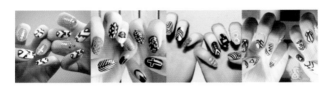

TRASH & READY
Nail art – Frederique Olthuis
www.trashandready.nl

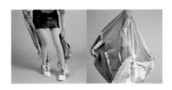

SIBLING
Walking Shelter – Sibling
www.tinanded.com.au

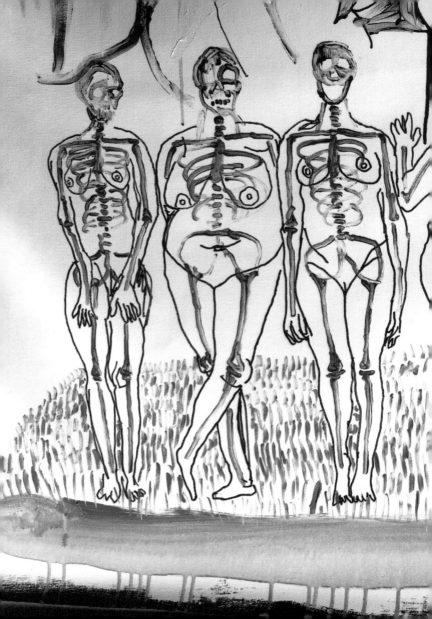